Plant Attack

Angela Royston

Ginn

Plants Bite Back

Most plants are harmless, but be careful – some plants like to bite back! They have special weapons to attack animals and people. But why do plants attack? Well, animals and people eat plants. Plants cannot run away, so some plants attack anything that touches them. So, wherever you go, watch out for plants on the attack!

As you stroll through these pages, write down and keep your answers to each **QUIZ** question. (Remember, the answers are in the book!) Okay? Bring on the plant attack!

What's Growing?

Sharp Spikes

Watch out for plants that scratch ...

PAGES 6 TO 9

Pretty, but POISONOUS!

Don't eat these plants!

PAGES 10 TO 13

Deadly poison

What a Stink!

cough!

Nasty Stings

Don't touch these plants ... they'll make your skin sore!

PAGES 16 TO 19

Meat Eaters

Insects beware... these plants will eat you!

PAGES 20 TO 23

CW00420901

Sharp Spikes

Some plants have prickly weapons – spikes or thorns! It is easy to tell which plants have spikes or thorns. You just have to look! The fish-hook cactus is covered with bunches of nasty spikes. The spike in the middle of each bunch is shaped like a fish-hook. The tip of this curved spike stabs into your skin. The hook stops you pulling it out again. **OUCH!**

The fish-hook cactus grows in deserts in North America. But anyone can grow them as pot plants, so watch out!

FiSH-HooK FaCT

The thick stem of a fish-hook cactus is full of water. This is just what animals in the desert are looking for – if they can only get past the sharp spikes!

7

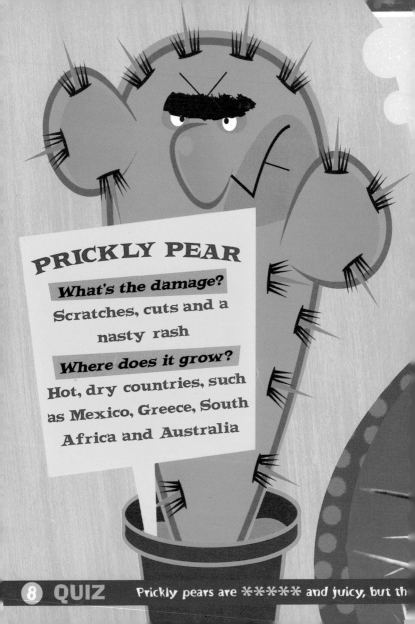

PRICKLY PEAR

What's the damage?
Scratches, cuts and a nasty rash

Where does it grow?
Hot, dry countries, such as Mexico, Greece, South Africa and Australia

Prickly pears are ✳✳✳✳✳ and juicy, but th

You can't get close to a prickly pear. It is covered with large, sharp spikes. If you get past the spikes, look out for the brown hairs. These aren't soft hairs – they have tips like fish-hooks that get stuck in your skin. So if you want to eat the sweet and juicy fruit of a prickly pear, get someone else to peel it for you!

Sharp spikes stop animals and people getting to the prickly pear's sweet juice.

Deadly Poison

Some plants contain poisons. If you eat them, they will make you very ill or even kill you. You cannot tell which plants are poisonous just by looking at them. Rhododendrons (say 'roh-da-den-drons') grow in many parks and gardens. The flowers and leaves look harmless. But do not put any part of the plant in your mouth. Eating just three leaves could kill you!

FaTaL FaCT

Rhododendrons have green leaves all year round. In winter, they look like a tasty meal to deer and other animals. But it could be the last meal they eat!

A rhododendron has beautiful flowers but the whole plant is poisonous!

This is what happens to someone who swallows a bit of rhododendron:

- Nose runs and eyes water (*not too bad so far*)
- Sore stomach (**ouch**)
- Vomiting (**yuk**)
- Can't breathe and can't move (**help!** *Now it's serious.*)

Long ago, people believed that mistletoe (say 'miss-al-toe') was magical. In winter, they tied mistletoe above their doors. They did this to protect their homes from evil spirits. Many people still decorate their homes with mistletoe at Christmas. And it is still used to make medicines. But whatever you do, don't try that yourself. The berries on mistletoe are very poisonous. They'd give you a **serious tummy ache!**

Are you trying to poison me?

Eating just three leaves from a rhododendron

In the past, people ate mistletoe to stop a poison working –

BIG

mistake!

What a Stink!

Rafflesia (say 'raff-ell-see-ah') will not spike you. It won't poison you either. But it smells so horrible that you will not want to go near it. Its flower smells like rotting meat. Flies love it! But don't worry – you would have to travel to the rainforests of South-East Asia to catch a whiff of this smelly plant.

Nasty Stings

FooD FaCT

Nettles are good for you! They can be made into a healthy soup or tea. Nettles taste like spinach (nice!).

When you cook nettles, they do not sting any more.

Dad, I think you need to cook them first!

Some stinging plants attack with spikes **AND** poison. You will soon know if your skin touches a stinging nettle. Stinging nettles are found everywhere. Their leaves are covered with tiny, spiky hairs. The hairs make your skin go red with white bumps. And your skin will **itch like mad!** But don't rub it – look for a dock leaf. Crush the dock leaf and rub it over the sting. It will soon stop hurting.

POISON IVY

What's the damage?
Itchy, stinging rash

Where does it grow?
Mainly in the USA,
but also in Britain

You can tell if a plant is poison ivy because the leaves grow in groups of three.

You will find poison ivy all over the place. It grows on walls, along the ground and up trees. The leaves of poison ivy make a nasty oil. If the oil touches your skin, it will give you a sore rash. The poison stays in the plant for a long time – even dead leaves will sting you! And the poison is so strong that the smoke from a plant on a bonfire can sting you too.

Meat Eaters

Some plants are really dangerous to insects. Why? Well, **the plants eat them!** One of these meat-eating plants is the pitcher plant. The leaves of a pitcher plant curl up to make a funnel. The funnel smells sweet. Insects follow the sweet smell and crawl inside. Then they slide down the slippery sides and cannot climb out. They fall into a pool of liquid at the bottom. **Splash!** The liquid slowly eats them up.

A pitcher plant is a death trap for insects.

Come in...

Pitcher plants grow in marshy ground. Most are quite small, but the yellow pitcher plant grows over a metre high. It is about as big as you!

A fly lands on a sweet-smelling leaf ...

Feed Me Flies!

VENUS FLYTRAP

What's the damage?
Kills and eats flies

Where does it grow?
In marshes and as pot plants

A Venus flytrap is a meat *****.

... Snap! The leaf closes and traps the fly.

When a fly lands on a Venus flytrap's leaf, it cannot escape from the spiky jaws. Juice in the leaves breaks the fly into tiny pieces. The tiny pieces mix with the juice and feed the plant. You can grow one of these meat eaters at home, as a pot plant. You have to feed the plant with dead flies.

So you've finished your stroll through the garden. Are you still in one piece? Did you find the answers to all the quiz questions? Now, juggle with the first letters of all five answers to make a sharp word that you have read in this book.

Poison

Ivy

Kill

Eater

Sweet

Juggle with the first letters SKPIE and you get... SPIKE! Ouch!